The American Revolution

Moments in History

by Shirley Jordan

Perfection Learning®

Cover Illustration: Sue Cornelison
Designer: Mindy Myers

About the Author

Shirley Jordan is a retired elementary school teacher and principal. Currently a lecturer in the teacher-training program at California State University, Fullerton, California, she sees exciting things happening in the world of social studies. Shirley loves to travel—with a preference for sites important to U.S. history.

She has had more than 50 travel articles published in recent years. It was through her travels that she became interested in "moments in history," those ironic and little-known stories that make one exclaim, "I didn't know that!" Such stories are woven throughout her books.

Image Credits: Art Today pp. 14 (top), 16–18, 19 (top), 26, 30, 43, 44; Essex Institute p. 14 (bottom); Library of Congress pp. 13, 19 (bottom), 33, 47; National Archives p. 51; I.N. Phelps Stokes Collection; Miriam and Ira D. Wallach Divison of Art, Prints and Photographs; New York Public Library ; Astor, Lenox and Tilden Foundations pp. 53, 55.

Table of Contents

A Timeline
of Important Events

1760 George III becomes King of England.

1765 King George III needs money to pay for his wars. His government, called Parliament, passes the Stamp Act. The people of the colonies must buy stamps to put on all goods. Angry, the colonists form the Continental Congress.

1770 British soldiers in their red coats are seen all over Boston. When the angry colonists want them to go away, the Redcoats fire their guns. Five colonists are killed in this Boston Massacre.

1773 Unhappy colonists stage the Boston Tea Party.

1775 British soldiers march toward Lexington and Concord. Paul Revere rides to warn the patriots in those two towns. George Washington is made general over the patriot army.

1776 The Declaration of Independence is written by the men of the Continental Congress.
In late summer, the Americans lose the Battle of Long Island. Many other losses follow.

1777 With the Americans almost beaten, George Washington and his troops suffer through the winter at Valley Forge.

1778 France enters the war on the side of the Americans. The French army and navy head for the colonies.

1779 John Paul Jones is a hero in waters off England's coast.

1781 After the Battle of Yorktown, Virginia, the British give up. The colonies have won the War for Independence.

1783 A peace agreement, or *treaty,* is signed in Paris.

Chapter 1

Tea Party for a King

The American colonists of 1773 loved tea. After all, their grandfathers had come to the new world from England. And in England, tea was the favorite drink. What did one offer a guest who came to call? A cup of tea, of course.

The citizens in the 13 American colonies were angry. For eight years, the British government, called Parliament, had been trying to raise money. A long war with France had cost the British a great deal. They wanted to get some of that money from the colonists.

So in 1765, they passed the Stamp Act—a tax on newspapers, legal contracts, and even playing cards.

"We won't pay it," the colonists cried. "We won't buy

goods from England. Then we won't have to pay their tax."

Bad feelings grew between the colonists and the British soldiers. Many wished the soldiers would go back home to England.

"Down with the Redcoats!" they told each other. "Send them back to King George!"

Boston, Massachusetts, was the city that gave the king and Parliament the most trouble. In 1770, an especially angry fight had broken out there. Before it was over, five patriot citizens were lying in the street. They had been shot dead by British soldiers. This terrible day was the Boston Massacre.

Samuel Adams was a leader in Boston. He wanted the British to leave. A few men had even heard him talk about independence. Someday, Adams hoped, the colonies would be free of the British king and Parliament.

Some wealthy and important friends agreed with him. They were John Hancock, Paul Revere, and Adams' own cousin, John. With other Boston patriots, they formed a group. From

then on, they would be called the Sons of Liberty.

And now there was this tax on tea! Angry citizens refused to buy it. Women gave "non-tea" parties. They only served milk or fruit juice. Some people even tried coffee. They would show King George!

The tax was three cents a pound. That was not much money—not even in 1773. But the colonists were tired of taking orders from a government across the sea.

Parliament gave the British East India Company the right to sell tea in the colonies. Late in the summer of 1773, the company sent ships to three port cities in America. They were New York, Philadelphia, and Boston. The ships were loaded with a total of 500,000 pounds of tea.

Paul Revere and other patriot riders rushed to their horses. Hurrying to all three cities, they spread the word. Most citizens quickly agreed not to buy tea. In fact, they would do more than that to oppose Parliament. They would refuse to unload the ships.

The plan worked in New York and Philadelphia. The British East India Company's ships sailed back to England. All the tea was still on board.

Things were different in Boston. For a long time, the British had known that this was the problem city. More action was needed. Now was the time to be firm with those colonists and their leaders.

Thomas Hutchinson was a rich Boston citizen. He was also the Royal Governor for the Massachusetts Colony. This made him England's person in charge for Boston.

Hutchinson put his trust in the king. He was a servant of Parliament. "These colonists must unload the tea," he ruled. "All the taxes must be paid."

But Hutchinson had another reason for his order. His two

sons worked for the British East India Company. They would make a great deal of money. But only if the tea was unloaded and sold in Boston.

In November, three ships sailed into Boston Harbor.

"It is just as Paul Revere said," said the men working on the docks. "Those ships are full of tea. See how low they are in the water?"

And the men working on the docks refused to unload them.

People from town gathered on the docks. As they looked out to sea, British warships sailed partway into the harbor. The guns on board pointed toward the docks.

Nothing happened for weeks. The people of Boston were nervous. They feared the British. They trembled at what might happen next.

Still, no one unloaded the tea. The East India Company's ships waited. The British warships stayed where they were.

At last, Governor Hutchinson took action. He set a deadline. The tea was to be off all three ships by December 16, 1773. The full tax must be paid by then. If these things did not happen, he would order the army to take over the ships and unload the tea.

It was a rainy December 16. The Sons of Liberty held a meeting in Boston's Old South Church. A crowd of 7,000 came. Time had almost run out. Some citizens crowded into the meeting to hear their leaders. Others had to stand outside.

One by one, the speakers talked to the crowd. They wanted the ships to return to England with the tea.

The crowd agreed. They grew angrier by the minute. Shouts rang out, "Down with the British! Down with King George!"

Suddenly, 50 men ran through the room. They wore blankets over their shoulders. They had painted their faces and bodies. They carried axes called *tomahawks*.

8

At first, the people thought they were Mohawk Indians. Then some sharp-eyed members of the crowd realized who they were. They were the leading citizens of Boston. Perhaps British spies would not know them in their Indian war paint.

The crowd was excited by the arrival of the fake "Indians." They shouted, "To the docks! To the docks!"

Everyone crowded out of the church and headed for the port of Boston. But when they got to the dock area, they became very quiet. No one wanted the men on the British warships to hear them.

Those dressed as Mohawks split into three groups. One

group ran to each of the ships filled with tea. They climbed aboard quietly.

When they ordered the sailors to open the cargo holds, no one argued. The crew members were not soldiers or sailors. They didn't want trouble. Who would risk his life to save a load of tea?

The crowd on the dock kept silent. There was no talking.

The tea was in chests—each one 320 pounds. The "Mohawks" broke open the chests. And they began to dump the tea into the harbor. Soon, other citizens of the town joined in.

In time, 342 chests of tea were floating in Boston Harbor. The men brushed the decks clean. There must be no tea left.

When they were done, the colonists marched back into town. They were so silent that the crews of the warships slept on.

Once back in town, everyone wore happy smiles. The people joked and danced. The Sons of Liberty and the people of Boston had given a fine party—

A tea party for King George!

When word reached Parliament in London, the British government took action. They could not prove which citizens had taken part in the tea party. So those people could not be punished as individuals.

Instead, the British decided to close the port of Boston. All of Massachusetts was placed under military control.

The colonists called these moves by Parliament the Intolerable Acts. People in the other 12 colonies were shocked. How dare Parliament treat Boston that way!

As a result, all 13 colonies ended trade with England. They elected representatives and formed the First Continental Congress.

Now the colonies would fight against British laws together.

 **10**

Chapter 2

At Home in 1776

A Typical Morning

"Ma!" Nathan pushed through the door with an armload of wood. "Wait till you see Jenny!" he shouted. "She's a mess!"

He went to the fire and peeked into the pot of cornmeal mush. It looked ready to eat. At 12, Nathan was always hungry.

Carefully, he piled more logs near the glowing fire. Smaller sticks and bark went into a basket. They would be used when the fire was very low.

His mother turned toward the door as Jenny stepped into the room. Jenny was Nathan's ten-year-old sister.

She held the front of her skirt in her hands. The cloth was in a tight bundle.

Her bonnet had slid to the side of her head. It covered one eye. She was dirty from her waist to her hem. A river of dripping, brown mud ran down her right side.

Jenny's eyes filled with tears. "Please, Ma, I can't go to school like this. When I went to milk Dolly, she wouldn't stand still. And by the time I finished, it was getting late."

Jenny wiped away a tear. "So I tried to gather the eggs in a hurry. And all the hens pecked at me. When the old rooster chased me, I ran and slipped in the mud."

She let go of her skirt. On the front was a yellow, gooey circle of broken eggs. The linen and wool cloth, or *linsey-woolsey,* was wet all the way through. Pieces of eggshell rolled down her skirt and softly plopped onto the dirt floor.

Mother sighed. Jenny should have worn her apron.

"Well," said Mother, "one thing's for sure. You can't stay home. School is too important."

She pulled a three-legged stool over to the fire. Then she picked up a wooden bowl from the table.

"Sit down here by the fire," she said. "I'll wash away the eggs while you eat. Just turn so the side of your skirt is near the heat. That way, the mud will dry."

Then she handed Jenny the steaming bowl of cornmeal mush.

Nathan couldn't stay quiet any longer. "Well," he fussed, "don't expect me to walk with her."

He saw his mother frown. But he continued anyway.

"I know she doesn't have another dress," he said. "But she should have been more careful. I don't want to be seen with her."

"Nathan!" Mother said sternly. "You are to stay with your sister as far as the Johnson house. Then she'll have Sissy and Betsy to walk with."

Mother rubbed a wet rag against Jenny's eggy mess. "And, Jenny, your skirt will dry while you walk. Just keep picking the mud away."

Jenny spooned up her mush. So far, this wasn't a very good day!

"And don't forget." Mother looked at both of them. "When

 12

you come home from school, we'll all pick apples.

"And, Nathan, you aren't working very fast on your knitting. You need those stockings. The ones you're wearing hardly reach from your shoes to your knees."

Mother smoothed Jenny's skirt. Then she said, "Off you go. Both of you."

You Are There

Did the above scene remind you of a typical morning at your house? Do you begin the day by milking the cow? Do you gather the eggs? Do you carry in firewood before breakfast? How many outfits do you have to wear to school?

Imagine that you are living in 1776. You live on a small farm—just like Nathan and Jenny—and just like many others . . .

Almost everything your family eats or wears is grown or made at home. And your house was built by your grandparents. They built it when they first cleared the land.

Your family grows corn, apples, squash, potatoes, beans, and pumpkins. There aren't any tomatoes, though. Everyone in town says those are poison.

The men and boys hunt rabbits, deer, and wild ducks in the nearby woods. Your family eats the meat. When the weather is bad, you have to settle for squirrels. But they aren't very tasty.

Your family owns a cow and some chickens. They have some pigs for meat and a sheep for wool.

Your mother tends a small garden of *flax*. That's the plant that linen comes from. She weaves linen yarn in one direction and wool yarn in the other. This is how she makes the strong cloth linsey-woolsey.

She uses this cloth to make clothes for the family. Linsey-woolsey is warm and useful. But oh, how it itches!

Your father makes shoes for you out of animal hide. You are lucky. Because he knows how to make the skins soft and comfortable.

He uses the same methods the Indians did. Some years, your parents are even able to save enough money to buy you a pair of shoes!

Shoemakers go from farm to farm. They make shoes for families.

14

Brand-new shoes, however, are not your favorites. Both the right shoe and the left shoe are the same.

It takes many months of wear before the shoes take the shape of your feet. Until then, they are not very comfortable.

Your town has a grassy square in the middle. It's called a *common.* It's also known as the *town square.* It  belongs to everyone. Parties and weddings are held there. And animals chew on the grass.

The men and women of your town spend much time at the common. They talk about freedom for the colonies.

One day last week, you walked by on an errand for your mother. You heard the men talking about King George. Everybody was angry about the taxes.

Your mother and her friends are definitely angry too. But they are angry about something else.

The king wants to send his English soldiers to live in people's houses.

Your mother says, "How can that work? No family we know has an extra room to give up. Besides, who wants to have strangers living in the house?"

Every week, there is a new worry about what King George might do. Parliament is so far away. It's in England. But they seem to pass new laws that affect you every few months.

Life in 1776 is hard to understand sometimes.

Chapter 3

Men Who Paved the Road to Independence

George Washington (1732–1799) is called the "Father of His Country." He led the Continental Army—the men who fought in the battle for freedom from England. People loved Washington. Many said he should be king of the colonies. But Washington said there had been enough trouble from kings. He would be a president. That way, the real power would stay with the people.

John Adams (1735–1826) was our first vice president. He served two terms under George Washington. Later, he became America's second president. When the U.S. capital moved from Philadelphia to Washington, D.C., Adams became the first president to live in the White House. His wife, Abigail, was its first hostess. Letters she wrote give us a good picture of life in the colonies.

Thomas Jefferson (1743–1826) was a fine writer who loved liberty. He was very involved when the colonies were ready to claim their independence from England. He wrote out his ideas. The other men of the Continental Congress changed many of those words. When all had agreed, the writings became our Declaration of Independence. In later years, Jefferson became America's third president.

Alexander Hamilton (1757–1804) was our nation's first Secretary of the Treasury. He served under George Washington. Hamilton organized the money affairs of the new United States. Hamilton believed in a strong national government. He often argued with others, such as Aaron Burr. Burr wanted the government to stay out of people's lives. On July 11, 1804, Hamilton fought a duel with Burr. Hamilton was badly wounded. And he died the next day.

 **17**

John Hancock (1737–1793) was a leader in the struggle for freedom. When the Declaration of Independence was finished, he signed his name boldly. The British wanted to arrest Hancock early on during the Revolution. But a warning from Paul Revere helped him escape safely.

Samuel Adams (1722–1803) was a patriot and leader in the fight for freedom. He was also John Adams' cousin. His speeches and writings stirred up the colonists' feelings. For this reason, King George wanted him arrested. With John Hancock, Adams was forced to run away. He was able to escape the British in Lexington, Massachusetts.

Benjamin Franklin (1706–1790) did many things well. He had been a soap-maker, a printer, and a writer. Everything around him held his interest. He made eyeglasses with two lenses. Today, many people read with *bifocal* glasses much like the ones Franklin invented. These glasses correct for both near vision and distant vision.

He proved that lightning was the same as electricity. He invented a stove to warm homes. Franklin played the violin, harp, and guitar. And he taught himself to speak five languages.

When the colonists needed him, he gladly became a leader for freedom. At the age of 70, he helped Thomas Jefferson write many parts of the Declaration of Independence.

He also helped get the French government to come to the

colonies and fight the British. This was perhaps his most important success during the American Revolution.

Benedict Arnold (1741–1801) was a brave American general. He led patriots into many of the war's most important battles. He often thought that the army should respect him more. He did not favor having the French join the fight. Near the end of the war, he turned against America.

Arnold began sending secrets to the British. When the Americans found out, he ran away. Escaping to New York City, he joined the British army. Benedict Arnold was our nation's first traitor.

John Paul Jones
The Hot-Tempered Captain

John Paul Jones was a hero in the American Revolution. He fought in the American navy for seven years.

The colonists were proud of him. But most of them never knew about his early years.

The life of a cabin boy was not easy in 1759. But it was the job 12-year-old John Paul longed for.

"I will work hard," he said. "Someday I might be an officer. Maybe even the captain of my own ship! For now, no job is too lowly. I will do my best."

During the next years, he rose in rank many times.

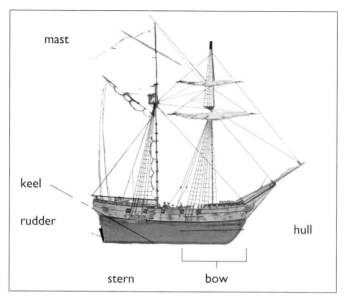

In 1768, he was 21. He was given his own ship to command. It was the *Betsy*. It set sail from Scotland, his native country. And it traveled between there and the unsafe, crime-filled waters of the southern Caribbean.

Young Captain John Paul was a skilled sailor. But he was a hard person to work for. Sailors on the *Betsy* never knew when his temper might explode. So they tried not to be noticed.

"If the captain doesn't see us, we're better off," they said.

The men gladly obeyed Captain Paul's orders. But they didn't have to like him!

Trouble Ahead!

Trouble came in 1772. The *Betsy* was on its second trip from an English port to the island of Tobago. Tobago was just north of South America.

You see, many of the men lived on Tobago. So they asked for their pay. Even though the trip wasn't over. But they wanted to be able to share the pay with their families.

Captain Paul stood before them. "You know what your

contracts say," he reminded them. "There will be no pay until the trip is finished. You may have your money when we are back in England."

The men knew the law was on Captain Paul's side. But they had seen other captains pay wages at the halfway mark. If they had to wait until the ship reached England, their children might go hungry.

"Sending the money back here to Tobago will take weeks," they argued.

The men grew angrier. They were sure their wages were on board.

"Our families need that money," they said. "Certainly our wages can be taken from the ship's strongbox."

The arguing continued. Soon, some of the sailors headed for the ship's *longboat*. That's a small, oared boat usually kept aboard a large ship.

Captain Paul had a terrible thought. To himself, he muttered, "Are the men going to desert? Are they leaving the ship? Without a crew, I will have no trading business at all!"

Paul seized a sword. And he ran after the sailors. He shouted warnings. His face twisted in anger.

The men stopped by the longboat. They were not sure what to do.

Just then, the tallest sailor picked up a heavy wooden peg. He turned back toward the captain.

Paul stepped back quickly, swinging his sword from side to side. He was forced backward, step by step.

At last, he was trapped against the main hatch. One step more, and he would fall deep into the hold!

The sailor lifted the peg high over his head. He was ready to strike.

Terrified, Captain Paul ran his sword through the man. The sailor fell dead.

Paul was shocked at what had just happened. He knew he should go ashore. Then he'd give himself up to the local judge, or *justice of the peace.*

Surely, the matter would be settled in his favor. He had been defending himself from harm.

Captain Paul Changes Course

But he changed his plans. Instead of reporting the event, he ran away.

He crossed the island and found another ship. It was ready to sail for England. He quickly ran aboard. In an instant, he was hidden among the other passengers.

Back at the *Betsy,* the crew was shocked.

"He wanted to turn himself in," his few friends said. "But he would not have found a fair judge in Tobago. He had to run away."

Paul would claim the same thing in later years.

Captain John Paul dropped out of sight for many months. When he was heard of again, he had added Jones to his name.

He still wanted a life at sea. So he went to the leaders of the American colonies. To them, a war on the sea against the British seemed close. They needed good and brave men if they were to fight King George.

John Paul Jones was named a first lieutenant in America's Continental Navy. The date was December 7, 1775.

Again the young man became a firm and angry leader. The officers in charge grew tired of his quarrels. And few men liked him. But one trait—his bravery—was never questioned.

During the American Revolution, he sailed a small ship, the *Bonhomme Richard.* He boldly crossed the Atlantic. He pushed right into the waters of the British Isles.

In 1779, Jones dared the English fleet to fight him. In battle

 **22**

BON HOMME RICHARD & SERAPIS

after battle, he showed what a brave leader he was.

Today, John Paul Jones is called the "Father of the American Navy."

Indeed, it would be hard to forget his fearless vow to the British: "I have not yet begun to fight!"

Paul Revere

"Down with the Redcoats. Down with King George!"

On March 5, 1775, many people crowded into Boston's Old South Church. They were there to honor five friends killed by the British.

The men had been shot down in the Boston Massacre five years earlier. Cries of "We must never forget them!" rang through the church.

No, they would never forget. The patriot crowd was angry.

Among the crowd was Paul Revere. Everyone knew him. He had spread the word about the ships filled with tea two years earlier. And what fine work he did with silver! His well-made bowls, pitchers, and tea sets were valued by many in Boston society. Everyone looked up to him as a leader.

He entered the church that day. His friends William Dawes and Sam Prescott greeted him.

"Come, Master Revere. Sit with us," they said. "We are

planning to get the word out. We think the Redcoats may march upon Lexington and Concord. We must spread the message to those two towns."

Samuel Adams and John Hancock were also in the church that day. King George wanted to send them to prison.

War Approaches

The threat of war was very real. If the British marched into Lexington or Concord, Adams and Hancock would slip away. They'd hide in the countryside.

How would the patriots know? They needed a signal. Revere, Dawes, and Prescott promised they would get the warning out.

British scouts had told the Redcoats that the colonists were collecting military supplies. Guns and bullets were hidden in the farm village of Concord.

The British commander, General Thomas Gage, decided to raid Concord. He'd take those weapons away.

General Gage wanted his Redcoat attack to be a surprise. So he ordered his men to walk slowly. No marching. He had them move along the Massachusetts roads as if they were in no hurry. They headed toward Lexington and Concord.

A huge British warship, the *Somerset*, sailed into place. It moved from Boston up the Charles River. It moved closer to the two small towns.

Anyone going to Lexington or Concord would have to get past that ship. With the *Somerset* in the way, no warning could reach those towns.

Six weeks passed. Paul Revere and his friends waited. They knew something was going on. And they were ready to take action.

 **24**

Revere had a plan. He knew what he planned was a crime called *treason.* He could be hanged. But Revere believed in freedom for the colonies. He was ready to risk his life.

On Tuesday, April 18, Boston's North Square filled with King George's Redcoats. They were ready for battle.

It's Time to Ride

At ten o'clock that night, Paul Revere received the signal to ride.

His wife, Rachel, begged him to be careful. "Your duty is to our large family. You must think about your own safety. And the future of our children."

She went on. "Couldn't someone else do this?"

But Revere would not change his mind.

Many years later, Paul Revere would tell his children about that night of April 18, 1775.

"I rushed from the house. I left the door open wide enough for our little dog Nipper to slip out. He followed me as I galloped away."

Revere hurried to the Old North Church. He was to arrange for a lantern signal.

His little dog caught up with him. Nipper followed his master to the riverbank, where two patriots waited with a boat.

"I knew there was danger in trying to cross the guarded river," Paul remembered. "The *Somerset* was blocking my way. On the far bank, another patriot waited. He held the reins of the best horse of John Larkin, the richest man in the city. I only had to get to the other side."

But Paul Revere made two serious mistakes that night. Perhaps he had rushed too much. Perhaps Rachel's tears and words had upset him. Perhaps he was just very nervous.

 **25**

Revere forgot to bring the cloth needed to wrap the oars. The cloth would have muffled their sound. The boat had to be very quiet as it slipped past the *Somerset*. There could be no splash.

And, worse than that—Revere had forgotten his spurs.

He would smile as he told the next part of the story to his children.

"I thought for a moment. Then I pulled a bit of paper from my pocket. I scribbled a note to your mother. Then I tied the paper around Nipper's collar. 'Go home!' I ordered."

Nipper and a Lady Save the Day

One of the patriots led Revere to a friend's nearby house. The man shouted up to the lady's upstairs room.

She came to the window. And the patriot told her what they needed.

The young woman wanted to help the cause of freedom. Quickly, she slipped off her flannel petticoat. Out the window it floated. Revere would later describe it as "still warm from the wearing."

 **26**

Running back to the riverbank, the three patriots spotted Nipper. He was just trotting back from home.

Rachel had read Revere's note. And around the furry messenger's neck hung his master's spurs.

The three men set out to cross the river. Silently, they rowed their boat past the *Somerset*. They were neither heard nor seen.

Before long, Paul Revere was riding valiantly toward Lexington and Concord. His dark head was bent, and his coat tails flapped behind him.

Little did he know he was riding into America's history!

Alexander Hamilton

"We will do our best," Alexander Hamilton said.

He looked at his group of 70 men. And he looked around their small fort on Manhattan Island, New York.

Then he said, "Don't lose hope."

Everything was going wrong. British soldiers were all around them. Hamilton could see the red of their coats on every hill.

Young Captain Hamilton and the other patriots could fight and die. Or they could give up. He knew what giving up would mean. The British would hang them all.

His men had not been soldiers for long. Some had left their farms to fight for freedom. Others had closed their shops.

Led by 21-year-old Captain Hamilton, these patriots had trained hard. Now they were true and trusted fighting men.

It was a very hot afternoon in August 1776. A whisper spread through the camp. One of the lookouts had just returned. He pushed through the crowd to Hamilton.

"British warships," he gulped. "I could see them all around us."

His hand went to his chest. He took a deep breath. "The

 27

king's army is now on the next hill. And his navy has taken over Brooklyn and Staten Island. We're trapped here."

Hamilton looked at his men's faces. He was not ready to give up.

"Is there no way out?" he asked.

"There might be," said the lookout. "I came upon one of General George Washington's scouts. The general has pulled his men back to the north end of the island. They're on a hill at Harlem Heights. About a day's march away."

"Could we reach them?" asked Hamilton.

"Maybe," the lookout said. "But we don't know the roads."

Hamilton sighed. He feared they were cut off from Harlem Heights. Cut off and surrounded. No one knew how to reach General Washington. Death seemed near.

The fighting had been quiet for some time.

The British must be getting ready, Hamilton thought. A new attack will come.

He gathered his men. "The British will surely attack soon," he said. "We are few in number. But we have a small chance. If there should be a heavy rain . . ."

The men looked at the clouds. Maybe, just maybe. Some of them gathered with friends to pray. It was very quiet in the camp.

The men did not sleep well. An attack could come at any time. But then a light rain began to fall.

Luck was with the patriots!

Sir William Howe, the British general, didn't like to make decisions. It would have been easy to wipe out Hamilton's men. But Howe did not attack. All evening, he thought it over. Now, as the rain grew stronger, General Howe waited some more.

Early in the morning, Hamilton heard some bad news.

"Our food is almost gone," the cooks told him. "It won't last the day."

28

Hamilton looked around the fort. In the morning light, tired men were starting to move about. They had no dry clothes. And no food for the day ahead.

Suddenly, the lookouts called an alarm. A rider was approaching. Was this the start of the final attack?

Full of fear, Hamilton rushed to the wall of the fort. He saw no army. There seemed to be just one horseman. In fact, the rider's uniform showed him to be a fellow patriot. He was an officer—a major.

The newcomer jumped from his horse. He was small and thin. And he was about Hamilton's age.

"You must get out of here!" he shouted. "The British outnumber you four to one. Follow me! I'll show you the way to rejoin General Washington's forces."

Then he began to march about the fort. Soon, he was giving orders to Hamilton's men.

Right away, Hamilton disliked the young man's bossy ways. But there was no way out of this trap. And they'd be of more value to General Washington alive than dead.

Quickly, the 70 men began to follow the young major. They marched out of the fort and up the road.

It was slow going. Their heavy cannons sank into thick, sticky mud. Even the summer rain felt cold.

Up a narrow trail they pushed. Then they turned along the west shore of Manhattan Island. Their feet slipped out from under them. Their boots slid into the wagon ruts. Sometimes, the rain was so heavy that a soldier couldn't see the man ahead of him.

It was daylight. But the British did not discover them. They marched nine miles north. They followed the young major to the safety of Harlem Heights.

General Washington's troops ran out to greet them. They

settled into the new camp. And they prepared to fight again for freedom.

Hamilton was thankful for the young major's help. But he didn't like him. This man was named Aaron Burr. And he and Hamilton would never be friends.

Maybe it was envy that came between Alexander Hamilton and Aaron Burr. Both had dreams of being famous. For years, they would both be important in America's government.

Hamilton became our nation's first Secretary of the Treasury. Eight years later, Burr became vice president under Thomas Jefferson. Over the years, they could never agree on anything.

Finally, in 1804, Alexander Hamilton used strong words against Burr.

Burr then shouted in anger. He dared Hamilton to meet him in a fight to the death with pistols—*a duel.*

There was really no way for Hamilton to avoid the duel. When they met, Hamilton raised his gun. But he did not shoot.

Burr took careful aim and fired.

At the age of 49, Alexander Hamilton died of a bullet in his side. He'd been shot by the very man who'd once saved him from the British.

Chapter 4

The Words of Freedom

Many people have never heard of John Dunlap. Nor do they know his place in America's history.

A printer in Philadelphia, Pennsylvania, Dunlap was known for his careful work on books and papers. In 1776, patriot Thomas Jefferson had a job for John Dunlap.

July 1, 1776

It was early on a hot Monday morning. Fifty men gathered. They had been chosen by the citizens of each of the 13 colonies. And they called themselves the Continental Congress.

It was time, they believed, to claim freedom.

John Adams, Thomas Jefferson, Benjamin Franklin, and the others hated King George's rules and taxes. They had talked about freedom many times. Now it was time to write down what they believed.

That Monday, they argued about what to do. Did they dare throw out a bad government? Did they dare try to drive the king's Redcoats out of their colonies?

John Dickinson of Pennsylvania was against leaving British rule.

"Independence," he said, "is like destroying our house in winter before we build another shelter."

Few others agreed with him. But he was a fine speaker. He talked for hours. The delegates listened to his words.

"The British will burn our cities!" he cried. "The Indians will join with the British! People will be murdered in the streets!"

John Adams argued back. His speech was long and powerful. When he was done, he called for a vote.

It didn't matter how many citizens had come to Philadelphia for the meeting. Each colony had only one vote.

Nine colonies voted yes. And four voted no. It was good— but not good enough.

South Carolina and Dickinson's state, Pennsylvania, voted no. New York *abstained*—they did not vote either way. They said they needed a message from home first.

Delaware's vote was a tie. Two members from that colony were present. One said yes, the other no. The third member from their colony was at home ill.

On Monday evening, the meeting ended. John Dunlap waited in his print shop. Thomas Jefferson had asked him to be ready.

July 2, 1776

The patriots from South Carolina talked most of the night. By morning, they had decided in favor of independence. Now they would vote yes.

New York again abstained. They would not vote until word came from their citizens.

John Adams was sure the sick patriot from Delaware would vote yes. He sent a rider to the man's home.

When Caesar Rodney read Adams' note, he saddled his horse and rode 80 miles to Philadelphia. A heavy storm flooded the roads. Trees fell across his path. Sick and wet, he arrived in time. He said, "Gentlemen, I vote for independence."

Everyone worried about Pennsylvania. Would John Dickinson hold out? Would that state vote no?

A surprise came that morning. Benjamin Franklin had been busy. Pennsylvania was his state too. He was loved and

33

respected by everyone there. And he had been able to persuade the other members from his state.

Dickinson was outnumbered. And he knew it. He never showed up at the Tuesday meeting. When the vote was taken, Franklin's voice was firm.

"Pennsylvania votes yes."

No one had voted no!

When John Dunlap closed his print shop that night, no word had come yet.

(A few weeks later, New York received authority to vote yes. The vote became 13 to 0.)

July 3, 1776

Now it was time to put the voting into words. Thomas Jefferson had already written his first draft. For many days, he had worked hard to find the right words.

The clerk read it through once. Then he went back to the beginning. The members could now suggest changes.

A sad Jefferson listened as the members of Congress talked. For hours, they changed one word, and then another. Sometimes they cut out a whole sentence. Jefferson looked tired. He sat in his chair and stared at the floor. He said nothing.

Arguments broke out when the part about owning slaves was reached. The members of Congress would never be able to agree on this.

Most of the men wanted the slaves to be free. In fact, Thomas Jefferson had already decided to free his.

But the men from South Carolina and Georgia said no. If the Declaration of Independence set the slaves free, those two colonies would not vote for it.

They demanded that part be crossed out. Southerners

depended upon blacks to do the hard work on their big farms, or *plantations.*

After much heated discussion, all words about slavery were removed from the Declaration of Independence. Now they were close to agreeing on the wording.

As July 3 ended, John Dunlap locked up his print shop. He had not yet heard from Mr. Jefferson.

July 4, 1776

On Thursday, the members of the Congress continued their work. They crossed out more sentences. And they changed a few more words. Jefferson frowned at each change.

Finally, the men considered the last part of the paper. It said that the new nation would be free. It would be independent from any other nation.

The men of the Continental Congress wanted everyone to know they agreed. Together, they formed the final words of the Declaration of Independence—

". . . we mutually pledge to each other our Lives, our Fortunes, and our sacred Honor."

Late that day, the Congress voted to approve the Declaration of Independence.

Now it was time for John Dunlap to go to work. Jefferson's copy of the Declaration of Independence was rushed to the print shop.

Dunlap gathered his helpers.

"We will have to work all night," he said.

He got out all his candles. Light danced on the walls as the printers bent over their work.

The copy in front of John Dunlap was messy. Words were crossed out. Others were written in. It was all very hard to read.

Dunlap held up a candle. He peered carefully at the paper. He read the words, one by one, to the workers.

Printing was known as *engrossing* in those days. Metal letters had to be arranged in the right order. Then they were set into a frame. Next, ink was spread across them.

When all the words were in place, the men got out sheets of paper. Each sheet was pressed by hand onto the inked plate of words. It was slow work. And very difficult to do by candlelight.

When the sun came up, the job was done. Dunlap and his men had made 100 copies.

Riders were waiting to carry them to each colony. The only men who had signed that first declaration were the clerk and John Hancock, president of the Continental Congress.

Copies of the Declaration of Independence spread across the countryside. John Dunlap had done his work well.

The People Hear the News

On Monday, July 8, the Philadelphia newspapers printed an announcement. The Declaration of Independence would be read aloud that day.

Later, the yard in front of the State House was jammed. At 12 o'clock, the huge bell on top of the building rang slowly.

John Dixon, a city leader, began to read. And the people cheered. They were free and independent!

"God bless the free states of America!" they cried. "Hurrah for our Declaration of Independence!"

Again, the bell in the tower rang out.

The bell was 23 years old. It rang all night in Philadelphia on July 8. People later began to call it the Liberty Bell.

The next day, George Washington sent out an order. The Declaration of Independence would be read to the soldiers in New York.

The soldiers and the citizens of New York were wild with happiness. They cheered and marched about.

"Down with King George!" they cried. "Long live freedom!"

That night, a group of people gathered in New York's harbor. They encircled a huge monument to the king. They hated that statue. It had been a gift from King George soon after he was crowned in 1770.

The statue was made of the finest lead. It was covered with gold. And it weighed two tons.

The figure of the king was dressed in a gown, or Roman *toga*. In his right hand was a staff, or *scepter*. This was a sign of his importance. The king was seated on a fine prancing horse.

The colonists built a bonfire. They threw ropes over the statue and began to pull.

The huge horse rocked and shook. At last, it toppled from its base. With a cheer, the people smashed it into pieces.

"Make it into bullet shells!" they shouted. "Then we'll shoot them back at old King George!"

They loaded the pieces into wagons. Then they moved them to Litchfield, Connecticut.

At the home of patriot Oliver Wolcott, the women of the town melted the metal into bullets. What a party they had!

The women filled the bullet molds repeatedly. Finally, they were done. They had made 42,088 bullets for General Washington's army.

Two More Printers

On July 19, 1776, John Hancock asked to have the Declaration of Independence printed again. This time, he wanted it on *parchment*. That was a rare, expensive paper made from a sheepskin.

Because of the cost, only one copy would be made that way. Hancock wanted it to be hand-lettered. He'd chosen printer Timothy Matlock of Philadelphia for the task.

Congress thought this was a grand idea. One member asked, "When it is ready, shall we not all sign it? We know there is danger from the king. But should we turn back now?"

The patriots agreed to meet again on August 2 for the signing.

Again, John Hancock made large, bold strokes with his pen. He wrote right in the center.

As he finished, he said, "There! His Majesty can now read my name without glasses."

After Hancock, the others signed. In all, 56 patriots signed the parchment copy. A few of them had not been in Philadelphia on July 4.

Another printer was important to the Declaration of Independence—a woman. Mary Katherine Goddard ran a print shop in Baltimore, Maryland. She was a brave woman who loved the cause of freedom. And she printed many copies of the document signed on August 2.

With Mrs. Goddard's help, the patriots wrote articles about freedom. And these were printed in her Baltimore newspaper.

Chapter 5

Weapons of War

America's success in the American Revolution was a surprise to many. Mostly to King George III.

You see, the colonists were not soldiers. Few of them had done any fighting at all.

England's Redcoats, however, knew about war. They were part of a trained army.

In the early years, the colonists had no uniforms. Each man carried whatever kind of gun he might own. There were few bullets. So the colonists melted pots and eating tools to make bullets.

There were few cannons or other large weapons in America. Earlier fighting in the colonies had been against the Indians. Cannons did not roll well over the rough ground. They would not fit between the trees in the forests, where the Indians hid.

In the Revolution, most fighting was done by the *infantry*, the men on the front lines of battle. The British Redcoats were

 **39**

well trained in this kind of battle. The Americans had no choice but to fight this way too.

In battle, both sides formed a battle line. Until everything was ready, the line stood still. They waited where the enemy cannons could not reach them. Then, when the order came, the men marched toward the enemy. Just like a parade.

When there was nothing else to use, the Americans carried hunting rifles. These were not a good weapon. They took too long to reload. And a knife, or *bayonet,* could not be fastened to the front of them.

After 1776, the colonists had uniforms and better weapons. But there weren't always enough to go around.

A fighting gun—the flintlock musket with a bayonet—was the main weapon of the war. These early muskets were six or seven feet long! And they weighed 40 pounds!

They were loaded from the muzzle with the soldier standing up. After each shot, the man had to reload. The *flintlock* was a metal wheel that turned and set off sparks. The sparks lit the powder in the barrel of the gun. A soldier carried extra gunpowder and lead balls in a leather shoulder bag.

Some officers had *breech-loading* rifles. These could be loaded from the side. Men with these fast rifles did not have to stand up to reload.

Hunting swords and small knives were worn by officers. A long, heavy weapon—the *saber*—was used by men on horses. These *cavalrymen* could reach farther from their horses with the saber.

American patriots who had no bayonets often used tomahawks. The Indians had taught them how.

40

Attack from Under the Sea

This might seem strange. But America's first submarine was part of the American Revolution.

David Bushnell was a young college student with a big idea. He knew the American patriots had few ships. And that the British navy was mighty. Perhaps, he thought, he could find a way to stop some of the British ships.

Bushnell built a special underwater boat of oak. It was shaped like a walnut. And it was big enough for a man to climb in and sit down.

The wood was wrapped with iron bands. Bushnell called his invention the *Turtle*.

To push it through the water, the man inside turned a set of blades, or *propellers*.

The plan was to get close to a British warship and drill a small hole in the side. Then the man in the submarine would stick a torpedo in the hole.

The torpedo was filled with gunpowder. After the *Turtle* left, the powder would blow up.

General George Washington liked the plan. The British had control of the waters around New York. If the Americans could blow up a few ships, maybe the frightened British would take their other ships away.

Bushnell chose the *Eagle*. It was the largest ship in the harbor.

On the day of the attack, David Bushnell was sick. So

General Ezra Lee was chosen to take his place.

Lee knew the plan. He would use a carpenter's drill attached to the front of the *Turtle*. He would stick the torpedo into the ship. And he would quickly set a timer. The blast would come after the submarine had moved away.

General Lee climbed into the *Turtle*. Quietly, he moved close to the warship. Now it was time to drill a hole just deep enough to hide a torpedo. He tried. But it wasn't working.

"Why won't this work?" he wondered. "I just know this ship is made of wood!"

Unfortunately, he had chosen a spot that was covered with copper. The drill would never go in. But Lee didn't know that.

The darkness of night was almost gone. There was no time to try another spot.

General Lee started back toward land. By now, sailors on the warship's deck had seen him.

The sailors said, "What is that strange thing just under the water?"

The *Eagle* sent out a small boat to see. Alarmed, Lee shot off a torpedo through the water. He did his best to aim it toward the ship.

He missed the *Eagle*. But as the torpedo exploded, water flew high into the air. Men on all the nearby ships began to shout and run about.

The British were terrified. They raised their anchors. Soon, all their ships were sailing out of New York's harbor.

The Redcoats had no idea what had attacked them. And they didn't know how many of the enemy there were.

The *Turtle* never sank any ships. But it showed that man could attack from underwater.

A new military weapon was born!

Chapter 6

Patriots in Petticoats

Abigail Adams was busy while her husband John met with the Continental Congress. She and her children could hear the boom of guns. But she stayed in her home. At times, she fed as many as 200 patriot soldiers who were camped nearby. In 1775, when metal was needed to make bullets, she quickly melted down her wedding spoons. She was the wife of America's second president. And she was the mother of its sixth.

Margaret Cochran Corbin fought alongside her husband. They fought at the battle of Fort Washington in New York. The

 **43**

man helping fire her husband's cannon was killed. And Margaret took his place. Later, her husband fell in battle. And she fired the cannon alone. Badly injured, she lost the use of her left arm.

Sybil Ludington has been called the "female Paul Revere." In 1777, her father, a colonel in the patriot army, came home for spring planting. Only a few men were left to guard the camp. Sybil's father learned of an attack by the British navy. He stayed home to gather the men. And she rode from farm to farm with the warning. The British were halted. And they ran back to their ships!

Lydia Darragh was a Pennsylvania housewife. She was forced to let British officers use her home. They met there for their evening meetings in 1777. One night, Lydia and her family had been ordered to go to bed. She hid in a closet and listened to British secrets. She heard about plans for an attack on General Washington's camp. Quickly, she slipped away on her horse. She rode 14 miles to warn the general.

Martha Washington was the nation's original First Lady. At one point, the colonists refused to buy British cloth for their clothes. They'd make their own. So she bought 16 spinning wheels. Each winter, she followed her husband to his winter headquarters. She was with him and the troops at Valley Forge during the terrible winter of 1777–1778. She faced cold and hunger along with everyone else.

Mary Hays helped her husband John fight the British. They were at Valley Forge too. Later, she and John fought in the Battle of Monmouth, New Jersey. John was shot. And Mary took over his cannon. She carried pitchers of water to the fighting men. So the patriots called her "Molly Pitcher."

Chapter 7

A Letter Home

Valley Forge, Pennsylvania
23 February, 1778

My dear Sarah,
By great good luck, I have found this bit of paper. It is a rare and prized thing. I hear there is no paper to be had. Not even for military messages.

How I have wanted to write to you. And if God wills it, these words will reach you safely.

I send love and good wishes to everyone at home in Virginia. Please hug the children for me. How I long to hold them! I send a kiss to each one.

General Washington says we are 25 miles from Philadelphia. Ah, fair Philadelphia! My heart breaks when I think of the Redcoats living the fine life in our capital city. How we fought them! There, and at Brandywine Creek.

 **46**

But success was not to be ours. Now we must fall back and camp here for the winter.

Valley Forge is a cold place. The snow is not deep, but the air chills us through. And we have a bigger problem. We have very little food. Hundreds have died from hunger and sickness, especially smallpox.

We have built simple log huts. I heard there are 900 of them—with 10 or 12 men in each one. At least the crowding helps us keep warm.

We each have a narrow bunk bed and a clothes peg on the wall. The pegs stay empty, however. To bear the cold, we must each wear all our clothes!

An old stone house was the only building when we came here. Everyone thought it would be for General Washington. But he stayed in his tent for many weeks. He refused to move to the house. Not until every one of his 1,100 fighting men had a roof over his head.

They say that 2,000 patriots here have no shoes. My boots have

holes. But I don't mind. I'm lucky to have my feet covered at all.

Last night a lookout put his hat down on the snow. Then he stood with his bare feet on the hat. If we were not so pitiful, it would have been a fine joke!

How we long for warm food to eat! Few supplies get through to us. For the Redcoats have blocked the roads. We hunt and fish when we can. Then we share with others in our cabin.

The people in the nearby towns are unfriendly. Some of them are Tories. They want us to obey the king. How they would like us to go home!

The others, I think, are afraid we might take their food. Indeed, a good meal would be welcome.

I don't know how the Prussian, Baron von Steuben, came to be here. They say George Washington made him a general in rank. We were not happy when he came. Who needs a general from across the Atlantic? we wondered. Our own officers can drill us! That was enough. But now I've changed my mind.

General von Steuben picked 120 men. He drilled them until they looked like real soldiers. He taught them to march in rows of four across. That's the way the Redcoats do it. Those first 120 men became leaders. Now they have gone out through the camp to teach others.

I think we will soon be a fine army. General Washington was wise to keep us together through the winter. And if we had not had more training, I think our war would be lost.

Last week, I learned how to fight with a bayonet. We had been using those weapons just for cooking.

Two Indians live in our cabin. From them we have learned to hunt and cook wild game.

At first, General Washington brought 400 Indians along to act as scouts. Now General von Steuben has taught them alongside us.

We may have even more help soon. Benjamin Franklin has

been talking to the French about joining us.

The Continental Congress says no blacks may serve in the army. They were pushed to that position by members from the South.

General Washington pays no attention to that rule. He says that any man who wants to fight for freedom is welcome in his army.

We have 3,000 black men here. As I write, two of them are on guard duty behind our cabin.

The gentle Martha Washington will move into the stone house next week. That brave woman stays with her husband at each winter camp. No matter how miserable the conditions.

How I long to have you here, dear Sarah. But what would become of our little ones? You, and they, are best off at home. Virginia is warmer. And I pray you have far more to eat than we do.

See how my scrap of paper has filled with words! It pains my heart that there is not more room.

A scout headed south waits for this letter. He'll start it on its way to you in Richmond.

Chapter 8

Benjamin Banneker and His Capital Ideas

Benjamin Banneker's Beginnings

In 1781, the patriots had many plans. They dreamed of a capital city for the new nation.

Had it not been for Benjamin Banneker, that capital might have looked very different.

 **50**

Benjamin was born in 1731 to a poor family in the colony of Maryland. He seemed to have little chance for success.

With his three younger sisters, he worked hard in the tobacco fields. The children hoed row after row in the hot sun or chilling rain. Then they returned home at dark to the family's plain shack.

Not only were the Bannekers poor, but their skin was black. (Benjamin's father and grandfather had both been freed slaves.) Both facts presented obstacles for the family. And they had to work very hard to overcome them.

Benjamin looked forward to the evenings. His grandmother, Molly, spent long hours with him. She told him stories and taught him to read from the family Bible.

The boy's hunger for learning grew. By the time he was five, Benjamin could read the words of the Bible with ease.

But what good did that do? There was almost no chance for a black boy to go to school.

Then a lucky thing happened for young Benjamin. A community of Quakers farmed the nearby land. Their church refused to worry about skin color. They were more interested in what was in the heart.

The friendly Quakers wanted the bright lad in their new school. Benjamin was the youngest student. And he was the only black boy.

Soon, he surprised the schoolmaster with how much he knew. Benjamin quickly moved up through the grades. At last, the teacher ran out of new books for the boy to learn from.

No More Fieldwork

When he finished school, Benjamin kept studying everything around him. Clocks were new in those days. And he was interested in how they worked. He borrowed a watch. Then he took it apart and studied the insides.

In the evenings, he began to copy the watch. He made the pieces much larger. He shaped the parts out of wood. And he studied his work until he had finished a fine clock.

It kept perfect time. And it sounded on the hours and half hours. People soon knew him as a man who could fix watches and clocks. He no longer had to work in the tobacco fields.

One day, George Ellicott gave Benjamin a simple telescope. George no longer wanted it. There were three books with it. They were filled with pictures of the stars.

Ellicott promised to stop by and explain these things to his friend. But Benjamin was in a hurry to learn. For weeks, he read the books by day. And studied the heavens by night.

Benjamin often went to Ellicott's store to meet with his neighbors. These men wanted to know the weather. So they could plan how to handle their crops. They wanted an up-to-date book about this. And Benjamin wrote one. This type of book is called an *almanac*.

Some famous men of science read the book. It was the best almanac they had ever seen.

But Benjamin Banneker's biggest adventure still lay ahead.

Enter Major L'Enfant

Now Congress had argued for more than ten years over which city should be our nation's capital. Boston, Philadelphia, and New York all wanted to be picked.

At last, Congress decided it should be a new city. It would

be on the banks of the Potomac River. The states of Maryland and Virginia agreed to give up the land. The city would not be in any one state. It would be called Washington, D.C.

The man chosen to draw up the plans for this new city was French. His name was Major Pierre Charles L'Enfant. He was very smart. But he could be hard to get along with.

He wanted to do everything *his* way. And he ran into trouble from the start. He could not work with the American leaders.

Major Andrew Ellicott was George Ellicott's brother. He was appointed chief *surveyor* for the new capital. It was his job to measure the land.

He began to choose people to help him. And he thought of his family's old friend, Benjamin Banneker.

At 60, Banneker was slowing down. (That was actually quite old in those days!) But he was pleased to be asked. Yes,

he said. He would help with this important job.

L'Enfant went ahead with his drawings. He often argued with the Americans in charge.

His plan for Washington showed city blocks laid out like a checkerboard. Wide avenues would cross the streets. At the center would be a capitol building on a hill.

Mud and hot weather made the work go slowly. L'Enfant became more difficult to work with. He shouted at the men.

No one could see his plans. Ellicott and Banneker were the only two people he trusted with his ideas. He showed them that streets named for the alphabet would run east and west. Streets with numbers went north and south. While the work was being done, L'Enfant's map was a secret.

Secretary of State Thomas Jefferson tired of L'Enfant. The man acted like a spoiled child.

One day, L'Enfant was unusually cross. He stormed out of his office. He took all his plans, notes, and records with him. He was off to his home in Paris.

Jefferson called a meeting of the staff. What would they do now?

A Great Mind at Work

Major Ellicott gave Benjamin Banneker a gentle push forward. Banneker quietly asked if the plans they had been using were good.

Jefferson nodded. He thought the plans were excellent. But now everything was gone.

There was no need for Jefferson to worry. In his head, Banneker held all the plans for the city of Washington, D.C. He could picture the streets and avenues. They would wind around Capitol Hill like spokes of a wheel. And he knew that the broad

54

main street, Pennsylvania Avenue, was to be 160 feet wide.

Banneker went home. He got out his own maps and journals. Next to them he spread out the few papers L'Enfant had left behind.

He began to draw and measure. He checked and rechecked. Within a month, he had drawn a fine new map for the city of Washington.

Slowly, the city took shape. Thanks to the ideas of a smart, but bad-tempered young L'Enfant—and the excellent memory of Benjamin Banneker.

Our nation was free. And now it had a home.

The site of the future capital as it looked in 1795.

Index